MW01248714

Sticks and Stones May Break Your Bones but Words Really Hurt Also

Marcus Hopkins

Trilogy Christian Publishers
A Wholly Owned Subsidary of Trinity Broadcasting Network
2442 Michelle Drive
Tustin, CA 92780

Copyright © 2024 by Marcus Hopkins

Scripture quotations marked (KJV) taken from *The Holy Bible, King James Version*. Cambridge Edition: 1769.

All rights reserved, including the right to reproduce this book or portions thereof in any form whatsoever.

For information, address Trilogy Christian Publishing
Rights Department, 2442 Michelle Drive, Tustin, CA 92780.
Trilogy Christian Publishing/ TBN and colophon are trademarks of Trinity Broadcasting Network.

For information about special discounts for bulk purchases, please contact Trilogy Christian Publishing.

Trilogy Disclaimer: The views and content expressed in this book are those of the author and may not necessarily reflect the views and doctrine of Trilogy Christian Publishing or the Trinity Broadcasting Network.

10 9 8 7 6 5 4 3 2 1

Library of Congress Cataloging-in-Publication Data is available.

ISBN 979-8-89041-280-5
ISBN 979-8-89041-281-2 (ebook)

Dedication

This book is dedicated to my children: Adriannie, Elijah, Cattleya, and Matias. Let my ceiling be your floor. To my wife for never letting me settle—there is no one I would rather go through this life with. And to my Lord and Savior Jesus Christ, for through Him all things are possible.

Saturdays are a day to relax after a long week of work and school. But things were far from calm and relaxing in the Hooper household.

"I'm telling Mom and Dad on you!!!" yelled Lulu as she ran into the kitchen from the backyard with her brother giving chase.

"Not if I tell on you first!!!" screamed Elijah.

"Mom!" both kids yelled at the same time.

"Elijah said I was slow as a snail." Lulu was five years old and daddy's little princess, but sometimes she forgot she was the princess, not the queen.

"Elijah, did you say that?" asked Mom.

"Well, she pinched me on my arm *hard*," replied Elijah. Elijah was seven and very patient, but he had to be with a little sister like Lulu.

GOAL!

3

"Elijah and Lulu, come into the living room," called Dad. As both kids raced into the living room, they saw Dad sitting in his favorite chair. "Take a seat, both of you. I want to tell you a story."

"See now we are in trouble," giggled both children.

"Growing up, there was a saying, 'Sticks and stones may break my bones, but words will never hurt me,'" said Dad.

"Why would you want to get hit by a stick or stone? That would really hurt," said Lulu.

"Yeah, Dad, and words don't hurt you because you can't feel them," said Elijah.

"When I was younger, this is how we would respond to a bully who was saying mean things to us. But son, words can hurt also, which is why I started saying, 'Sticks and stones may break my bones, but words hurt also,'" replied Dad.

"Can I tell you a story about the power of words? This story began when I was in fifth grade. This was when I met my best friend, Aaron. He and his family had just moved from Chicago. We became friends because we both loved basketball and watching a certain great basketball player from Chicago. Aaron would stay at my house almost every weekend, and we became best friends. I wondered why he liked staying at my house so much, and one weekend, I got the chance to stay at Aaron's. I was excited, but Aaron…not so much.

'What are you doing in there?' yelled Aaron's mom.

'Mom, I'm sorry we broke the light; it was an accident,' pleaded Aaron.

'Are you stupid? Can you ever do anything right?' replied Aaron's mom.

"That was the first and last time I asked to stay at Aaron's house. Things were not only tough for Aaron at home, but school wasn't much better.

'Now raise your hand and tell me what you want to be when you grow up,' said Mr. Lane. 'Mindy, what do you want to be when you grow up?'

'I want to be the first female president,' replied Mindy.

'Mark, what about you?'

'I want to play football for the Detroit Cats,' said Mark.

'And what about you, Aaron?'

'I want to be a doctor,' said Aaron nervously.

"A loud *ding* sounded the bell for lunch as we raced toward the door.

"Aaron and I were still gathering our things when Mr. Lane came over.

'Aaron, can I talk to you for a second?' said Mr. Lane. 'Maybe you should try to be something other than a doctor.'

"At lunch recess, we would play basketball. *Clink* was the loud sound the basketball made as Aaron's shot slammed off the backboard and rocketed to the ground.

'Aw man, we could have won! Why did you pass it to him? He never makes it,' Cole, one of the mean boys, said to Aaron.

"Over time, I began to see my friend change. He stopped coming over as much and started hanging with the wrong crowd. One day I saw Aaron hanging out with his new friends and wanted to invite him to the movies.

'Hey buddy, you want to come with me to see the new superhero movie?' I asked.

'That movie is dumb; you are such a baby. Me and the fellas are going to watch that new scary movie,' laughed Aaron and his friends as they walked away.

"*Ouch*. It felt as if Aaron had hit me in my stomach. I had never been hit by a stick or a stone but it was at this moment I realized how much words can hurt. I couldn't get Aaron off my mind; I needed advice, so I went to get help from the one person I knew had the answer—God.

17

'Hey Lord, I need your help. I feel my friend Aaron is hurting and in need of help. I don't understand how a person can change like that. It's like he became what people were saying about him—'

'The problem is the words spoken to him,' Pastor Hilts told me. 'I heard you praying from the other room. Words are powerful, Mark. God used words to create the world when He said, "Let there be light," and it was so. Words can build a person up or tear a person down. The Bible also says, "as a man thinketh in his heart, so is he" in Proverbs 23:7 in the KJV version. The words people have spoken about your friend are in his heart. So, we need to get the bad words out of your friend's heart and get good words in.'

'Thanks, Pastor.' I had a plan as I ran home.

"The next day I put my plan into action. While playing basketball at lunch, it was my day to be captain.

'I'll take Aaron with my first pick.'

'Dude, what is with you? Are you trying to lose? You should have picked someone better.'

'No, I have taken the best player here,' I said.

'What are you talking about, man? I stink.'

'As I said, I've taken the best player.'

'Do you believe that I am the best player?' Aaron asked me with astonishment.

"We will be discussing that lunch game when we are old men in retirement homes. It was not only the best game I was a part of at Reed Elementary School, but it was the best game I saw Aaron play. He couldn't miss. I saw the light back in my friend for the first time in a long time. I even talked to my teachers, and they wanted to help out.

"Aaron later told me Mr. Lane had pulled him aside after class one day. He said he wanted to apologize for his comments the other day and that he thought Aaron could do whatever he put his heart to. Mr. Lane said he thought Aaron would make a great doctor one day.

"And you know what? Aaron eventually became a doctor.

22

"I even talked to his parents; surprisingly, they understood because the same thing happened to them when they were little. Both of their parents told them they would never do anything with their lives.

'We love you, son, and think you are so special,' said Aaron's parents as they hugged their son.

'Thanks, Mom and Dad. I love you too, and you are the best parents,' cried Aaron as I watched him hug his parents.

"Aaron even started attending church on Sundays; soon after, his parents started attending.

'John 3:16 says, "For God so loved the world that he gave his only begotten Son, that whosoever believeth in him shall not perish, but have everlasting life," (John 3:16, KJV) preached Pastor Hilt.

'You hear that, Mom and Dad? God loves us,' I heard Aaron say.

"These are the greatest words we need to hear and the words that matter the most—the words that express what our Heavenly Father thinks about us. So, what do you kids think?"

Both kids were fast asleep on Dad's shoulders.

"I never get tired of hearing that story," said Mom from the kitchen doorway.

"And I never get tired of telling it," chuckled Mark.

"And while you were talking, Aaron called and wanted to see if you were still coming over to watch the basketball game."

"I'll call him back right now."

The End

Printed in the USA
CPSIA information can be obtained
at www.ICGtesting.com
LVHW070037120524
780010LV00013B/186